Introduction

Why is a new edition Henry Schradieck's "The School of Violin Technique" being published at this time? The answer to that question is the positive experience that generations of excellent teachers and students have had with this work.Therefore it is to these experiences that this work is still recommended for intensive study in the development of basic violin technique. The applicability of this work is proven by the excellent workmanship by the author, who in brief musical phrases - with simple movement examples - gradually progresses to more and more complex and challenging combinations full of lively musical invention.

This technical progression enables (according to the individual abilities of the student), already from the beginning of instruction, a granting of the study of this work. Gradual technical difficulty forces us, according to our own needs, to more and more challenging intepretations which in the final phase should cover the intentions of the composer completely. In this is given the main point which, in individual steps of the study, should not only not be left out, but focused upon:

1. Before we start the actual study of individual exercises, we devote – particularly at the beginning of study – utmost attention to the efficient relationship between body and instrument. This is:
    a) correct posture,
    b) setting the instrument on the body with a balanced placement of the instrument,
    the left arm, thumb and fingers so that the greatest freedom of movement is ascertained.
    c) mutual coordination of the left and right arms for their optimal effectiveness in playing.
2. At each development level, but particurly at the beginnings, we begin with a slow, freer tempo allowing us – through listening – to achieve the best intonation and sound clarity, always with targeted and appropriate motoric activity.
3. At beginning level of study we may also start with the use of bowing and rhythmical variations. While working on those I emphasize not forgetting the fundamental character of the music's content. For the rhythmical variation, I suggest dotted rhythms and the exchange of a quadruplet for an eighth note with a triplet and vice versa, or:

Bowing variations of detaché, martelé, staccato and spiccato should be used. When practicing complicated string crossings, (ex: No. 4 & 9) we can temporarily employ – also for final performance – legato in 2,3,4,6,8 and 12 notes with the use of various parts of the bow. Never forget about the freedom and flexibility of the wrist.
4. Taking in consideration distinct articulation and sound clarity of technical performance, in some circumstances, I modestly propose different fingering solutions. I suggest similar changes in cases of difficult extensions which increase tension in the left hand and affect intonation and sound clarity. My own fingering proposals are marked below the notation, the author's original fingerings above.
5. I place a significant emphasis on exercises in high positions which, particularly, in advanced stages of instruction, are qualitative stabilizers of sound and intonational success. We can never overestimate the importance of the functional effectivity of the right hand, mutual coordination of both arms and the well-balanced position of the body.
6. The final result in performing each sequence, at every level of instruction, in every step of individual maturity of technique should be, above all:
    a) rhythmically clear
    b) agile in tempo (not at the expense of quality)
    c) distinct in articulation
    d) clear in intonation and sound
    e) a musically alive (imaginative, personally improvised) interpretation of each exercise.

Simply, this should all come from point "e)" and be demonstrated, in each sequence, in "concert performance." In no case should the final "music making" change into spiritless finger exercises and lose the final effect of the success of the performed work.

Jaroslav Foltýn, Prague

Henry SCHRADIECK (1846 – 1918); was an exceptional violinist and teacher, from a Hamburg musical family. He was a student of Ferdinand David (1810-1873) in Leipzig and Hubert Leonard (1819 – 1890) in Brussels. He was a concertmaster and teacher in Germany, Russia and America. His "School of Violin Technique" (Die Schule der Violintechnik), published in 1875 in Hamburg was produced in three independent parts, Volume II containing exercises in double stops and Volume II, exercises for the right hand. Since its original publication, the Volume I has proven to be the greatest success in teaching practice.

1

Exercises on one string

Henry Schradieck
(1846 - 1918)

2

4

4   Exercises to be practised by the wrist
only keeping the right upper arm
perfectly quiet

5   Exercises on three strings

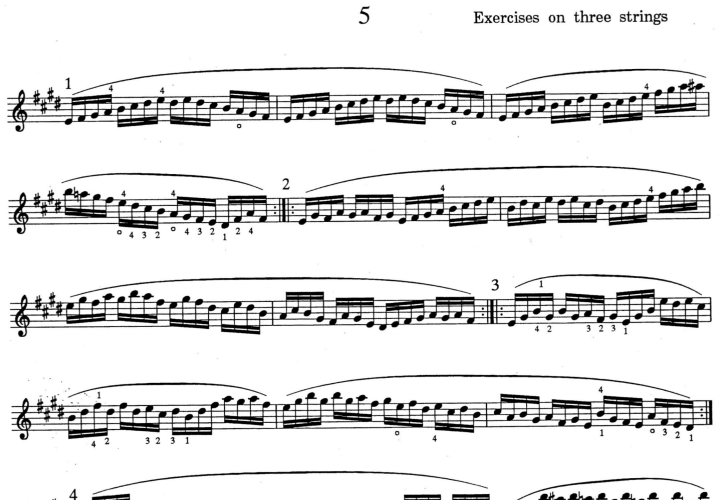

6

Exercises on four strings

CODA

12

9

Exercises in the first and second position

13

10

Exercises in the third position

11   Exercises in the first, second and third position

16

12

Exercises in the fourth position

18

13

Exercises in the first, second,
third and fourth position

20

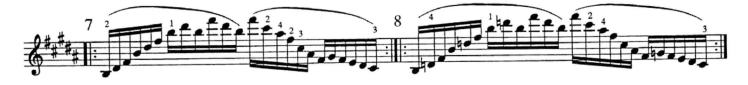

15

Exercises passing through five positions

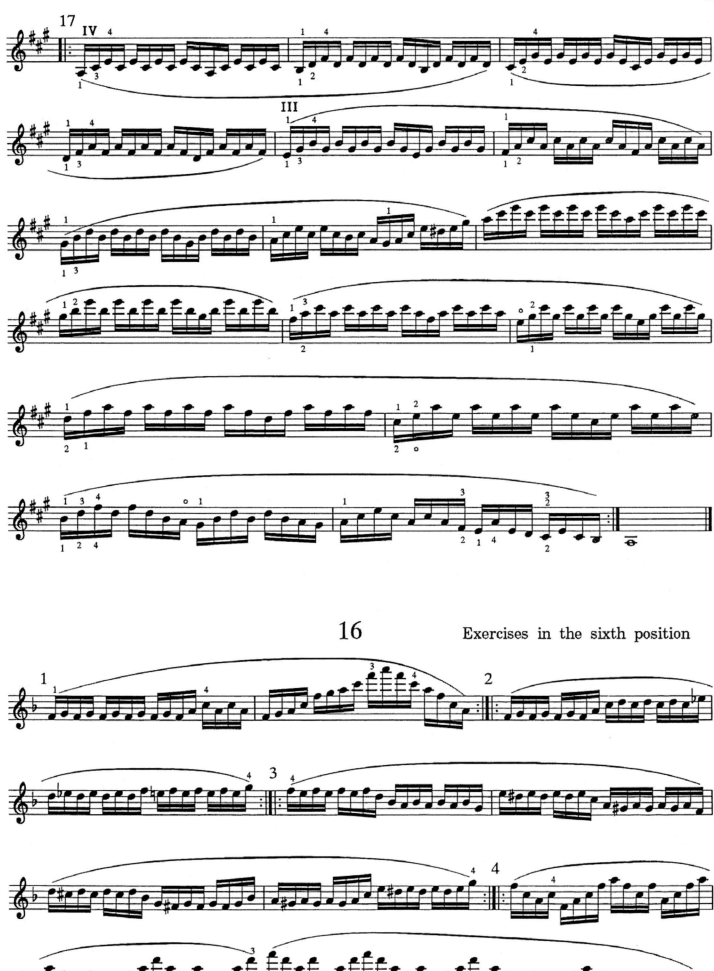

23

16   Exercises in the sixth position

24

17   Exercises passing through six positions

26

18   Exercises in the seventh position

28

19 Exercises passing through all positions

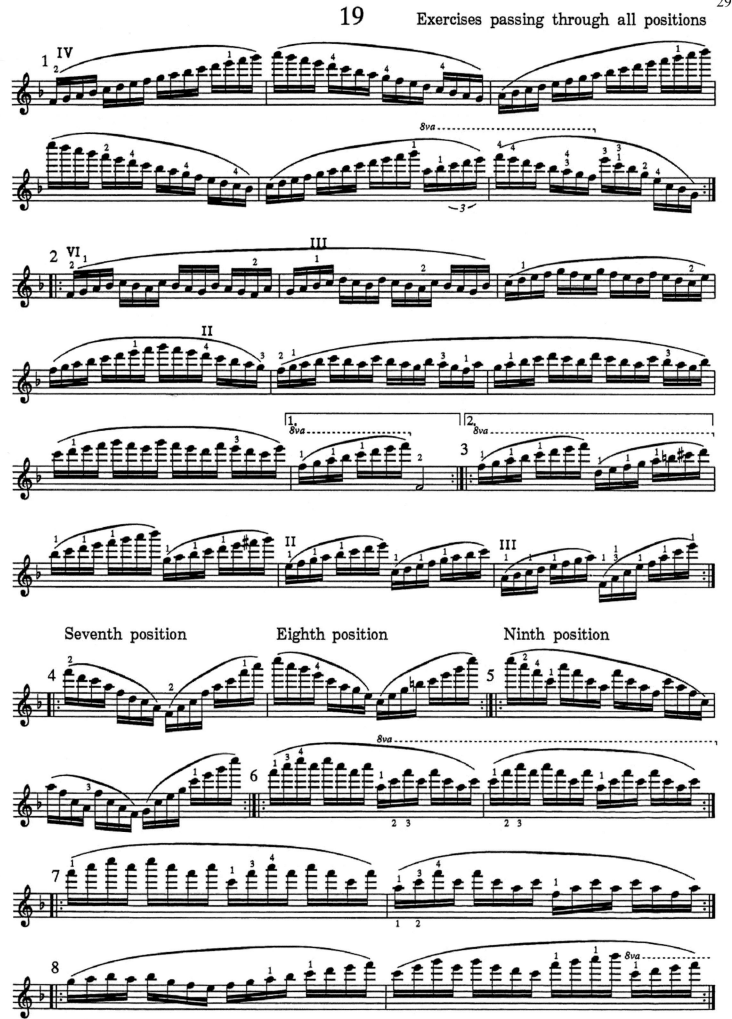

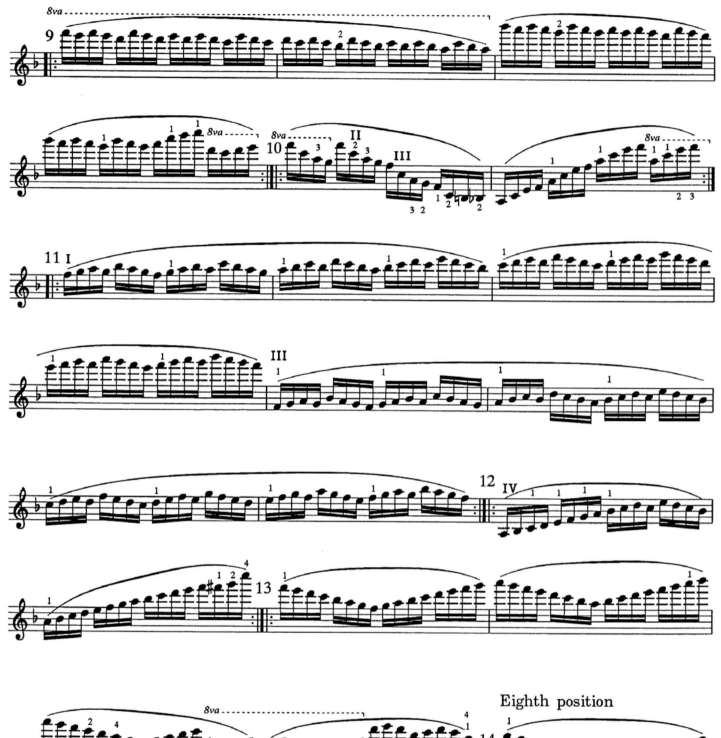

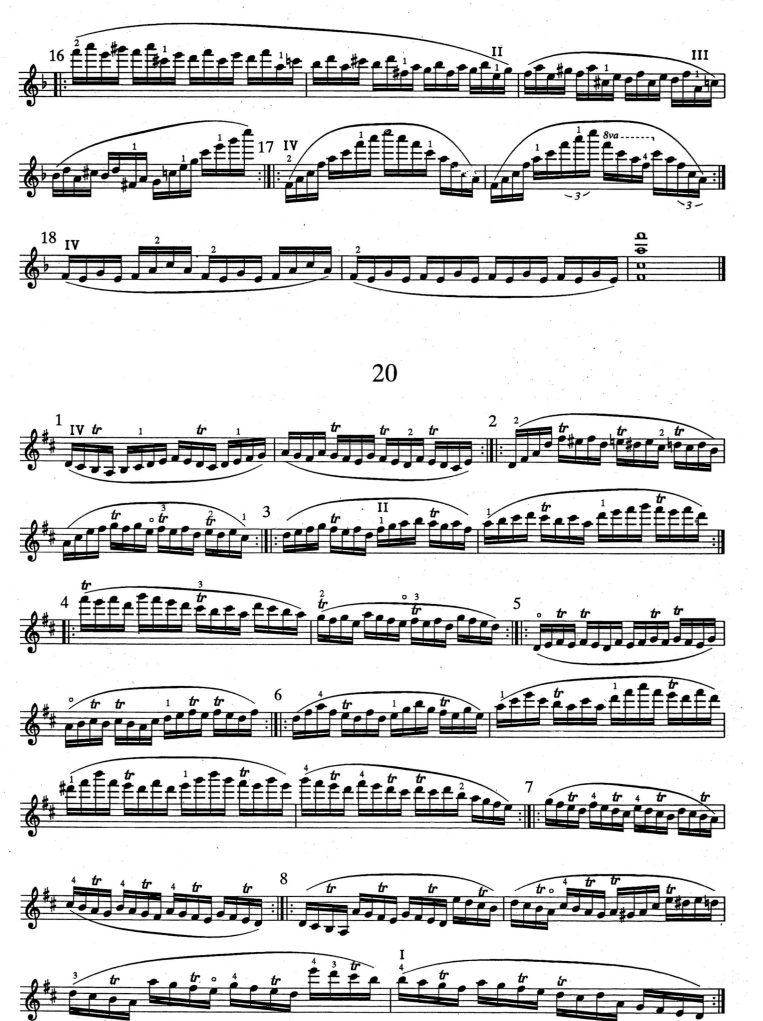

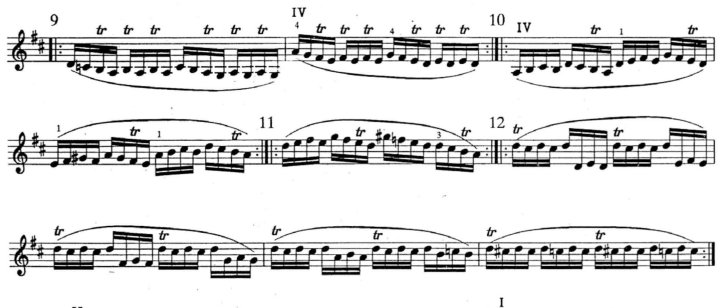